DREAMS

INTERPRETATIONS,
HIDDEN MEANINGS,
SYMBOLS

DREAMS

INTERPRETATIONS,
HIDDEN MEANINGS,
SYMBOLS

ALISON DAVIES

ILLUSTRATIONS BY
JESÚS SOTÉS VICENTE

Hardie Grant

QUADRILLE

Contents

Introduction

We are near waking when we dream we are dreaming.
NOVALIS

The universe of dreams may at first seem complex, offering up starry landscapes and alternate worlds. It's a place of self-discovery; a magical realm where you are the author of your own destiny. Everything you see and experience is your creation, and while it may be unchartered territory, it is built on your thoughts, feelings and beliefs, so ultimately there is nothing to fear. To step inside you only have to drift into dream. In this slumber state the reins of control are relinquished and your subconscious takes the lead. When we are awake our conscious mind is in charge. This is both practical and present, taking the lead and helping us make the most of each day. The subconscious is a very different master with a much lighter and surreal touch, who does not stamp authority using rules, but instead allows you, through the power of dream, to tap into deep and often forgotten reserves of creativity.

Dreamland is an ethereal vista, a place of imagination and mystery where anything goes. Your mind, which while awake is often full of details and worries, becomes a blank canvas, waiting for you to express yourself in a fusion of colour. Dream time is an opportunity to play, experience and explore, and although anxieties that plagued you in the day may still appear, this is your chance to work through them and make sense of the world.

In the pages of this book learn how to crack your own dream code, decipher the symbols and befriend your subconscious. Discover the deeper meanings behind common dreams and learn that nightmares can turn out to be hidden gems in the war against fear. There's a comprehensive guide, which includes a variety of dream scenarios and how to interpret them. With stunning imagery and a smattering of stardust, you'll enter a sleepy otherworld and emerge brighter, and with a renewed love for the phenomenon that is *your* dreams.

Decipher your Dreams

Step into the nonsensical world of dreams and enter
a surreal landscape where upside down and back to front are
commonplace. Snippets of stories are interlaced with potent
imagery, and the backdrop continually shifts, making for
a sometimes disconcerting yet often memorable experience.
It's no wonder we become so confused by our dreams. How
do you create order from something so random and reveal
the deeper meaning? The answer is simple; you can crack
your dream code by taking a step-by-step approach, applying
a degree of logic and a sprinkling of imagination.

Dreams are a personal thing. Two people might share the
same dream but their response and the resulting perspective
is unique depending on their background, life experience
and situation. The first step to decoding your dreams is to
immediately jot down what you can remember and how the
dream made you feel. Your initial reflections are guided by
intuition, which comes directly from the subconscious mind,
the same place your dreams reside.

Crack the Code

Putting the bare bones of the dream on paper provides a starting point as well as hooks from which you can slip back into the dream and relive parts of it. This will help you conjure up the emotions that you experienced. How you felt is extremely important, as this gives a clear indication of the deeper meaning. If you felt angry and frustrated during the dream, then it makes sense that the frustrations have been carried over from your waking world. You need to be honest about the source of your annoyance and you'll begin to see how this ties in with your dream.

While many dreams reflect what you're going through in real life in some form, there are also dreams that deal with hopes, fears and deep-seated desires. These often feel more vivid and real, because they are issues that are close to our heart and embedded in the psyche. This explains why nightmares can stay with us for days. Dreams like this may be mistaken as premonitions of the future, when in fact it's just the subconscious speaking to us on a primal level.

Understand your Dreams

STEP ONE

◇ How did the dream make you feel? List the emotions that you experienced. There may be more than one, particularly if the dream was constantly shifting.

◇ If you could summarize the dream in a sentence what would you say? Take this a step further and imagine you only had one word to describe the dream, what would it be?

◇ Write everything down and read through your thoughts.

STEP TWO

◇ Make a list of the people, places and things in your dream.

◇ From this list, circle any symbols that stood out.

◇ Consider each symbol and what it means to you. What does it represent, in a few words? Write down your thoughts.

STEP THREE

◇ Read through the list of emotions and symbols. Can you see a pattern? Is there anything to connect the symbols and emotions?

◇ If you can piece together a narrative, consider whether it reflects something that is happening in your life.

◇ Even if you can't come to any definite conclusions, continue to note down your dreams for the next few days, and see if similar emotions and symbols arise.

Follow this process and over time you'll better understand the language of your dreams and what specific symbols mean for you. This will give you an insight into your dreams and you'll learn to trust your intuition, whether sleeping or awake!

Common Dreams

Deep into that darkness peering, long I stood there,
wondering, fearing, doubting, dreaming dreams no mortal
ever dared to dream before.
EDGAR ALLAN POE

Dreams are very much an individual thing, but there are
common dreams that we all experience from time to time.
The human psyche is made in such a way that we have similar
hopes, aspirations and fears, despite our unique personalities.
These act as triggers within the subconscious, conjuring up
dream scenarios that are universal. These narratives bring
different emotions to the surface, helping us play out and
work through desires and fears while we sleep.

Dreams are a way of making sense of the waking world, so
if you're going through a particularly stressful or challenging
time, then you might experience one or more of these
common dreams. While each one has a consensual meaning,
they are still personal reflections of how you think and feel,
so always start with your initial response and then consider
the general interpretation and how it relates to you and what
is happening in your life.

Falling

It is thought that every person will dream of falling at least five times in their life. The source of this narrative stems from insecurity. Just as in the dream, we have no control of the situation and find ourselves plummeting downwards, there's a sense of losing control in the real world. You may feel overwhelmed emotionally, mentally or physically. Events have spiralled, and you feel anxious about the outcome. If you find yourself hanging on in some way, this suggests that you're still trying to maintain your grip on reality. The more you struggle in the dream, the more you're fighting the situation.

Look to your surroundings for more specific clues, for example, if you fall from an office block window and you currently work in an office, this hints at career chaos and disappointment. If you plunge headfirst into water, then this relates to your emotional life, and it could be a personal relationship that is causing you distress. Dreams of falling also indicate a sense of failure. Ask yourself, why do I think I have failed? What could I honestly have done differently? Remember that every experience good or bad, has something positive to teach us.

Drowning

If you feel like you are drowning in a dream then you are most likely drowning in real life in some way. You could be drowning in sorrow, overwhelmed by your emotions for something or someone, or drowning in debt. You feel like you are in 'over your head' and that you cannot breathe. Often this refers to a relationship, because the element of water is linked to the emotions. In this instance, you could be in too deep and feel you've lost your sense of identity. There's a sinking feeling that comes with this, you find yourself in a difficult situation and you don't how you're going to get out of it. Stay calm. Breathe and spend some time in quiet contemplation. Give your brain the oxygen it needs to come up with a practical solution.

Flying

Flying in a dream brings with it a sense of freedom. It is usually an exhilarating, joyful experience, where the dreamer feels on top of the world. One of the most positive common dream narratives, it is an auspicious sign, suggesting you feel not only in control of your life, but also happy with the way things are going. Often related to attainment, flying can signify the achievement of a goal or cherished wish. Depending on your skill as a flier, you could be soaring ahead in your personal and professional life.

An alternative interpretation suggests you've managed to rise above something that has been bothering you. You're free of worry and able to move onwards and upwards. If you've grown wings to help you fly, this suggests a period of spiritual growth. You will learn much about yourself and reach new heights of wisdom and understanding.

Losing Teeth

Since the second century people have dreamed of losing their teeth, and there are countless written accounts that substantiate this. While the ancients believed this was an omen of death, the reality is much simpler. If your teeth fall out, then you're most likely to be going through a highly stressful period in your life. Rooted in anxiety, this dream can make you feel vulnerable, but in fact it's exposing your current vulnerability and reflecting the sense of loss you feel about something in your waking world. It can be a dent to the ego, as teeth are an integral part of our facial structure. In this instance it suggests you may have lost face in some way, either personally or professionally.

This dream could also indicate you've lost something which is dear to you, and you're going through the grieving process. Either way this dream, though deeply upsetting, is a sign that you are working through things; you are undergoing a transitional period and will eventually emerge, stronger and brighter.

Being Chased

This is another common dream based on fear and anxiety. If you find yourself being chased by something or someone, whether known to you or not, then you are probably feeling vulnerable in your waking life. You could be under pressure and feel that time is running out, or you are actually avoiding a problem or situation and trying to run away from it. Ask yourself, what do I fear? What am I trying to avoid? You might have already put some distance between yourself and the thing that is causing you anxiety, but if the pursuer in your dreams catches up, then this suggests you will eventually meet matters head on and that this is the only way to rectify the situation.

If you are the one doing the chasing, this denotes an ambitious personality, someone with drive who will not take no for answer. There is still a sense of pressure – in this case you desperately want to reach your goal and panic may be setting in. Take a deep breath and accept that sometimes you cannot force matters, you simply have to go with the flow and let life lead you in new and exciting directions.

Being Naked

Finding yourself naked in a dream can be a shock: perhaps you were going about your daily business, at work or walking down the street, and suddenly you notice your clothes are missing! You are exposed, and this is exactly what you fear in your waking life. There is something you have been hiding; this could be an aspect of your personality, a secret, or something you feel ashamed of. You're afraid that this is about to be revealed.

It could be that you feel all eyes are on you at this time and you're fearful of doing or saying something wrong. Naked dreams are common when we feel under pressure to perform: at an interview, in a test or giving a presentation. Look to your dream surroundings for clues as to which area of your life this is pointing to. Also notice how others look at you. If they fail to notice your nudity, then this suggests your fears are unfounded and you are letting them take over rather than focusing on the task in hand.

Naked dreams can be extremely liberating, particularly if you feel confident without clothes! This suggests that you are happy in your own skin and feel able to reveal who you really are to the world.

Needing and Going
to the Toilet

To dream you desperately need the toilet and either cannot
find one, or they are all in use, or have no doors or locks,
suggests a need to let go of something. While you may
already know what this is, you don't know how to approach
it and you are struggling to express your emotional needs.
Going to the toilet is a process which helps us eliminate
toxins, and when we can't do this in our dream or find
ourselves doing it in strange situations, this indicates a need
to release something that is unhealthy for us. Toilet training
starts at an early age, it is part of growing up, so dreams about
using the toilet can take us back to childhood. You could be
feeling small and as if your needs don't matter. It's time to
speak up and put yourself first.

Nightmares in General

Generally, nightmares come from a range of emotions, including anxiety, guilt, confusion and stress. If you are going through a tough time in your life, then you're more susceptible to this type of dream. Depression is another cause, but while stress is a major factor, other things can trigger these types of emotionally charged dreams. Eating late at night, consuming too much caffeine and even certain medications all produce nightmares. If you continue to be plagued by the same dream and it's affecting how you feel in your waking life, then try and change the narrative. You can do this by bringing the dream scenario to mind, but instead of letting it play out in a negative way, change the ending so that it becomes positive – in other words, the monster turns out to be friendly and only wants to play. Repeat the positive version of the narrative every day, running through it in your mind and over time the original nightmare will dissipate.

Recurring Dreams

At certain periods in life, we might experience the
same dream several times over. Otherwise known as
a recurring dream, it can be as regular as every night, or
three or four times a month. Usually when this happens
we're going through a transitional phase. Something has
upset the status quo, leaving us feeling unsettled and the
recurring dream is our way of dealing with the changes.
The dream itself may be pleasant or disturbing and it's
a good idea to look at the actual symbols involved as well
as the emotions to find a clue to the deeper meaning.

Some people experience an entire series of dreams in
sequence. Again, it's a good idea to identify the underlying
narrative and what it might reveal about your life. For
example, a story that outlines two people, falling in love and
eventually getting married, might suggest the dreamer is
looking for a of 'happy ever after' ending in real life.

The Symbol Guide

Trust in dreams, for in them is hidden the gate to eternity.
KHALIL GIBRAN

There are millions of dream symbols and scenarios, and this number grows every day. Being as unique as we are, it would take a lifetime to list them all. To help you on your journey into dreamland this guide features some of the key concepts and imaginings from the sleeping mind. It provides a starting point from which you can begin to unravel your dreams. Each symbol has a variety of interpretations drawn from psychology and folklore. Take your time and find the one that feels right for you or make up your own.

FOOD
&
RECREATION

◇◇◇

There is no sincerer love than the love of food.
GEORGE BERNARD SHAW

Cooking

There's an element of care in cooking as you are taking the time to prepare a meal for yourself or for others. Of course, the real proof is in the pudding; is the meal an edible delight, or a disaster? If it is the former, then you can expect success when it comes to plans or projects you're implementing now; if it is the latter, then you'll still reach your goal, but must apply yourself and learn from your mistakes.

Dining Out

To dream you're enjoying a nice meal in the company of friends or family, is a positive sign. It suggests that there will be pleasurable times ahead, and you'll be able to share your good fortune with those you love. What happens during the meal and how you feel also has some bearing on the meaning. If the meal ends in tears, consider how this happened, was there some kind of miscommunication? Look to your waking life, and how you can communicate better to avoid misunderstandings with your nearest and dearest.

Eating

We eat to nourish our body, so dreams of eating often indicate a need to take care of ourselves. Look at your diet and see if you can make any positive changes, consider your health and well-being in general.

What you eat and how you are eating it is also important. If you're munching on your favourite treats, then this could mean you're craving comfort; while ravenously gobbling down food means you are hungry for something in real life. Ask yourself 'What is missing from my world? Where do I feel lacking?' If the food makes you sick, then this is a clear sign that something in your life is making you feel bad. Find out what it is and get rid of it.

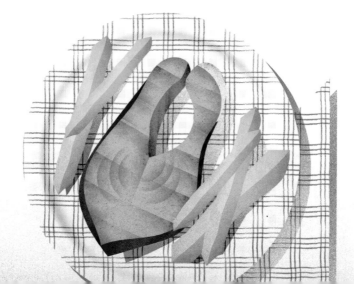

Types of Food

Food comes in all shapes and forms, and just as you can eat almost anything in life, the same goes for time spent in dreamland. Here are some common food symbols and a summary of their meanings.

APPLE

Often linked to romance in folklore, dreaming of this fruit could indicate a new love interest on the horizon. If you are taking a bite this suggests you feel tempted in some way.

BANANA

Associated with fertility, eating a banana suggests a period of abundance and productivity.

PEACH

A positive symbol associated with peace and happiness, the juicier the peach, the more joyful your experiences in daily life.

PEAR

Considered a good omen, eating a pear is a sign that success is on its way. You could be lucky in love or business!

POTATOES

This root vegetable is associated with sustenance and prosperity; if you dig them up in your dream, this suggests you'll make your own luck. To eat them means you are likely to find the financial security you seek.

CARROTS

Associated with health and well-being, to see or eat a carrot in your dream indicates you'll soon be feeling on top form. Also linked to love, carrots can suggest a romantic interlude is imminent.

OTHER VEGETABLES

All vegetables are associated with health and eating them can mean you need to attend to your diet and general well-being. If you've been ill recently, it's a sign that you'll be feeling better shortly. Green leafy vegetables suggest a need for healing.

MEAT

Eating meat shows a need for nourishment; this could be in a physical sense, or on an emotional or spiritual level. Also associated with money, it can indicate a cash windfall or that you need to get your finances in order.

FISH

A highly spiritual symbol, eating fish suggests you are evaluating your beliefs. You may be going through some kind of transition. This is generally a positive sign.

CHEESE

If you're snacking on cheese in your dream, then blessings in your waking world are on their way. These will be associated with money and security.

MUSIC
&
LEISURE

◇◇◇

If music be the food love, play on …
WILLIAM SHAKESPEARE, TWELFTH NIGHT

Playing an Instrument

To dream of learning to play an instrument suggests a sense of purpose and a need to apply yourself. You could have a project in mind or something you're already working towards and you know it will take time and effort. There's a sense of balance and harmony that comes with anything musical, and it may be that to progress you need to listen with an open heart, and then you'll find your groove.

Consider the instrument you're playing, as this has some influence on the meaning. If you're using your hands, this suggests a need to be practical, whereas a woodwind instrument might indicate a need to take a deep breath and find your voice to move forwards. If you're an accomplished musician, then this translates to your waking world where you'll be met with the recognition you deserve.

Listening to Music

One of the greatest pleasures in life is in listening to a tune and getting lost in the melody. It doesn't matter what the song is, if you're enjoying it then you're in the moment. Consider how you felt during the dream. Did the music lift you up, or bring you down to earth? If you can remember what it was make a note of the title, as this could be a clue to the underlying message. One thing is obvious, this dream is urging you to take a step back, become aware of your surroundings and really listen to what others are saying.

Writing Music

If you're composing music in your dream it's
because you're feeling creative in real life. The urge
to produce something of worth has bubbled to the
surface in your dreams. To see yourself performing
or conducting an orchestra, suggests you aspire
to create something of value that can be appreciated
by others. Consider your talents and skills and how
you can use them to fulfil your passions.

Dancing

The release of swaying your body in time with music is incredibly primal, and something humans have done for millennia. There's a sense of freedom that comes with any type of dance, and the ability to abandon inhibitions and let go is liberating. The core message of this dream is that you need to cut loose somehow, relinquish constraints and find the independence you seek. It's time to express yourself and get in touch with your wants and needs. Fun times are ahead so put your best foot forward!

Watching TV

Watching TV is something we tend to do to relax and unwind. It's an activity we can do solo or with others, but the main focus is the screen. Where does your attention lie at this moment in time? This dream is asking you to find your focus. If you already have something in mind, be sure it's worthy of your attention. Consider too what you were watching in your dream and how it made you feel. For example, a scary programme relates to your fears, but something that made you laugh suggests you need to see the funny side of life.

FITNESS
&
EXERCISE

◇◇◇

Exercise is labour without weariness.

SAMUEL JOHNSON

Running a Marathon

Unless you're actually planning to run a marathon in real life, this dream is quite simple to decipher. You've a goal in mind, you have it in sight, but it's going to take hard work and tenacity to reach it. Falling while running suggests a need to find your feet and steady any nerves. Don't worry if you don't reach the finish line or feel you can't go on, this is your subconscious helping you work through any fears that might hinder your progress while you sleep.

Walking

A steady walk soothes the soul and has the same effect in dreamland. If you're in an environment that is unknown to you, then you'll soon be exploring pastures new; this could be in the form of a new job or moving home. If you're in the countryside enjoying nature then this is highly positive and indicates a period of peace and harmony. You'll feel inspired and at ease with life over the coming weeks.

Exercising

Working out requires effort and determination, even in slumber. The type of exercise you choose, reflects what you're going through. Pumping iron suggests you're weighed down with responsibility, but if you see yourself lifting those heavy weights then it's a sign that this period is almost over. You will prevail! A fast and furious exercise class depicts a chaotic mind. Streamline your to-do list, by prioritizing and channelling your energy, and you'll sail through workouts, in life and the dream realm.

Swimming

Do you dive in at the deep end or descend steadily into the watery depths? How you approach the swim says a lot about how you're feeling in general. A bold leap suggests an optimistic and adventurous attitude, whereas the opposite shows you're in cautious mode. If you're in a pool, then consider its shape. If it's square or rectangular, a logical, practical mind is at work; if it's circular, then you could be looking for a sense of completion. Water babies taking to the ocean are freedom seekers who refuse to be confined by rules or regulations; they are looking for space in some part of their life.

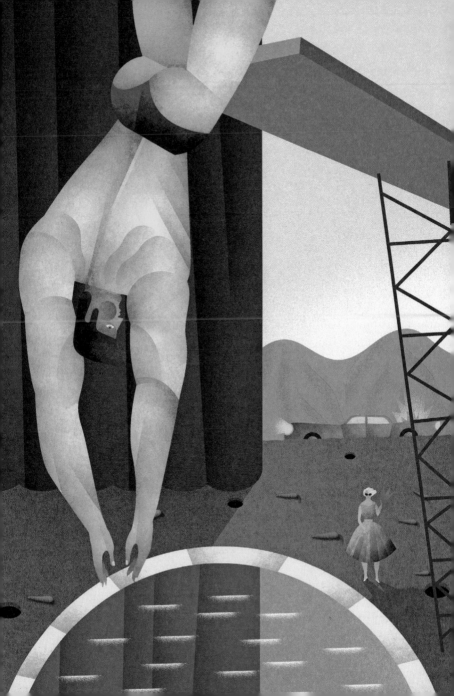

FASHION
&
LIFESTYLE

◇◇◇

I don't do fashion. I am fashion.
COCO CHANEL

Catwalk

Gliding down the catwalk with all eyes on you might be heaven for some and a nightmare for others. The meaning of this dream is dependent on how you felt at the time and what happened. If you were confident then you enjoy the limelight, and this translates to daily life where you could soon be taking centre stage. If you were uncomfortable, then you need to retreat in some way. Your behaviour is under scrutiny. The conveyor belt nature of the catwalk means that whatever you're going through will soon pass.

Modelling

Models have a certain image to portray and that's how you feel too. If you dreamt you were a model, then you've set yourself a standard or you're trying to live up to someone else's ideals. Depending on how you felt during the dream, this can be a good or bad thing. You might be striving to do something better, or simply feel under pressure to look or act in a certain way.

Clothing

To dream of an item of clothing, whether you are wearing or buying it is significant, depending on what it is. Footwear relates to how grounded you feel, and if you're secure in yourself. Glamorous heels suggest a need to be elevated and admired. Practical styles reveal a solid, dependable nature. Trousers mean business with a capital 'B', while a gorgeous dress is about self-confidence and sexuality. Headwear is often linked to spirituality. If it is delicate, then there's a joyful lightness to your presence. A warm, woolly hat suggests a comforting person who looks out for others.

Sewing

Sewing is something we do either to make something to wear, or to repair something. Dreaming of sewing suggests you need to work hard to create something or make it better. It can often refer to a relationship and mending some kind of rift which that has occurred. If you're sewing with a machine, then the reconciliation you're hoping for is on a much larger scale than if you're sewing by hand.

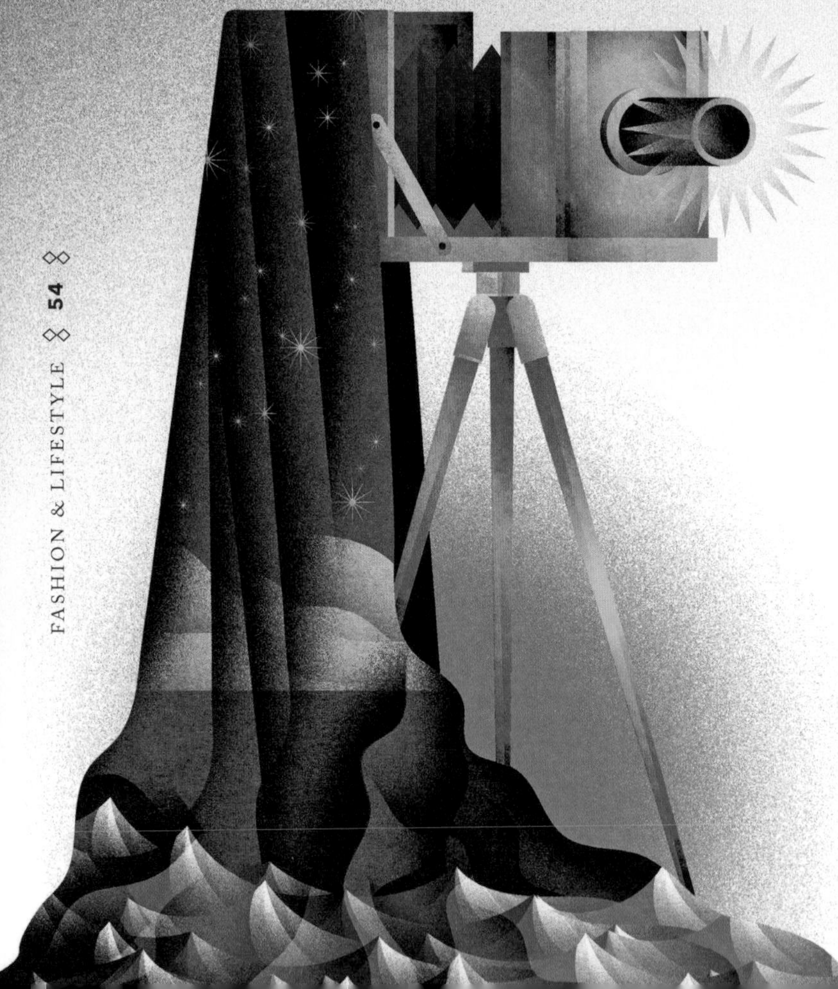

Photography

If you are the one being photographed in the dream, then you could be feeling drained and at the mercy of others in your daily life. It seems that everyone wants something from you, and while the attention is flattering, after a while it becomes a chore. If you are the photographer then there is something you're desperately trying to hold on to. It could be a feeling, a memory or something physical that you're trying to capture.

Hobbies

Doing what you love in a dream is always a positive sign. You feel happy with who you are, and where life is right now. Look at the skills involved in this pastime. If it's practical and craft-related, then whatever you've been building in real life, whether that is a family, business or another dream – keep going, you are on the right path. If it is something active and sporty, then there's a competitive element which gives you the edge.

Famous People

Dreaming of someone famous is aspirational; there is something about this person that you identify with, or perhaps you'd like to be in their position. If they treat you like a friend, there's a degree of acceptance; socially you want to feel part of the group. If they're off hand and dismissive, it suggests a fear of rejection. This could be from a new partner, friend or someone you hold in high regard. To dream you are famous means you're yearning for recognition. Don't worry, this dream is a sure sign you're about to get your moment in the sun!

Royalty

To dream of meeting royalty suggests you're looking to impress someone. You want to please them in some way and gain their respect. If you dream that you are royal, consider the position you hold: king or queen tends to mean you'd like to take charge and command more respect; prince or princess suggests a need to be put on a pedestal. Ultimately you are craving adoration.

TRAVEL

◇◇◇

Travelling expands the mind rarely.
HANS CHRISTIAN ANDERSEN

Different Countries

Dreaming of other countries is a definite sign that you need a break. You've been working hard, and your subconscious is telling you to ease up, relax and take some time out. Change is afoot! Consider the country in your dreams and what it means to you. Have you been there before, and if so, how did it make you feel? If it's somewhere you've never been, then it's time to step outside of your comfort zone. Change your routine in some way and reignite your zest for life.

Holidays

Dreaming you're on holiday is an obvious sign
that you're craving change. This could be a change
in your surroundings, a new job or some kind of
personal transformation. Holidays are to be enjoyed
and there's a sense of fun about this type of dream,
which suggests pleasant times ahead. If the holiday
turns sour in some way, then you may have some
reservations about the changes you'd like to make.
You're worried you'll regret taking the leap. Have
faith, take each day as it comes and trust that
you'll make the right decision.

Culture

Taking in the culture of a new place is exciting. You look at things through fresh eyes and that's what this dream is all about, finding a different perspective. Whether you're visiting a historical building, making friends with the locals, or exploring the city streets, you'll be open to each experience. You're being urged to look at something in your life in a new way. Once you start to do this, happiness is yours.

Hotels

Hotels provide temporary accommodation, they're a stopgap and a place to rest your head during your journey. If one pops up in a dream, then the underlying message is that whatever situation you're facing in daily life, it's only temporary. It's part of a process that you have to move through. If the hotel is plush and luxurious, this suggests a period of pleasure and attainment, if it's plain or even prison-like, then it indicates a difficult and constrictive phase. Either way, this is just a cycle and it's coming to an end.

Caravans

A caravan is a portable home and something you can take to any location. When it turns up in your dreams it suggests that family is important to you. You could be craving the comfort and love of those who know you best or missing them in some way. You feel disconnected from your nearest and dearest. Whatever is causing the distance between you, this dream is urging you to reconnect and sort out any minor disputes or misunderstandings.

Tents

Whether you're a camping fan or not, the presence of a tent in your dream indicates a feeling of impermanence. You are in a situation that does not feel secure, and while it might serve you at the moment, eventually it will become surplus to your needs. It could be that you're longing to put down roots in some way, but it's not the right time. If the tent blows away, then this suggests things will come to an end shortly and you'll be able to move on.

Luggage

Luggage in dreams represents the emotional baggage you carry with you. To lose your luggage can be a sign that you need to let go of something which is causing you stress. While the reality of lost luggage is upsetting, this dream also suggests there's something or someone you're not comfortable with. If you can barely pick up your luggage then your subconscious is telling you to drop it, cut the ties that bind you to the past and move forwards with an open heart.

Passports

Passports identify us and seeing one in your dream suggests you're finding out who you are and learning something new about yourself. To lose your passport is like losing a part of yourself, this could be because of a difficult situation or ongoing struggle. To see your passport stamped suggests you're looking for approval in some way.

Aeroplanes

Being a mode of transport associated with far-off places, or to watch one take off in your dream indicates a need for escape. You long for pastures new, and a fresh start. If you're a passenger and the journey is smooth, then you could see your ambitions soar, you're about to make a huge leap in progress. If your flight is fraught with turbulence then you could hit some challenges along the way. Even so, you're on the way to achieving your dreams, so like any good pilot keep your destination in mind and enjoy the journey.

Cars

Often seen as a status symbol, your choice of car is
a personal thing. If you find yourself driving one in your
dreams, it shows how you see yourself and how you'd
like others to view you. Something sleek red and sporty
belies a sassy nature; while something black and powerful
suggests a self-assured person who likes to take the lead.
Consider what the type of car means to you. If you're racing
the car or speeding in some way, then you're likely to be
impatient about something that's occurring in your life.
You desperately want to move things along and this
sense of frustration is coming through in your dreams.

Boats

Setting sail is an exhilarating experience. The ocean is vast and can take you anywhere. Dreaming you're at sea can mean you feel slightly lost in real life. Perhaps you have too many options and don't know which one to take. If you're drifting in a boat out of sight of land, then you have no direction or sense of purpose; but if you're heading for a specific location then you're primed and ready to seize the right opportunity. Cruising on an ocean liner suggests a desire for luxury. An unexpected trip, or holiday could also be on the cards.

Trains

A train in your dream is a sign that you're going places. If it's going too fast, then this suggests that something is out of control in your life. It could be that you feel events have been thrust upon you, and you're struggling to keep up. If the train journey is pleasurable and you feel safe, then it's a positive sign. You are on the right track.

Bicycles

You need strength and stamina to ride a bicycle for any length of time. Whether you're hitting the city streets, or travelling over rough terrain, energy is required and that is the meaning of this dream symbol. You can get to where you want to be in life, but you need to make the effort. Don't expect things to land in your lap. Instead actively pursue your dreams. You're being given the green light. Go for it but be prepared to work hard to get the results you want.

Motorbikes

Super speedy and dynamic, there's something adventurous about riding a motorbike: it is fast, furious and can get you where you need to be in a heartbeat. There's also an element of risk. To dream you're riding a motorbike suggests you're looking for more excitement in life, or you're in a rush to succeed. Either way, there's a sense of urgency. While you might be feeling impatient, remember the old adage 'fools rush in where angels fear to tread'.

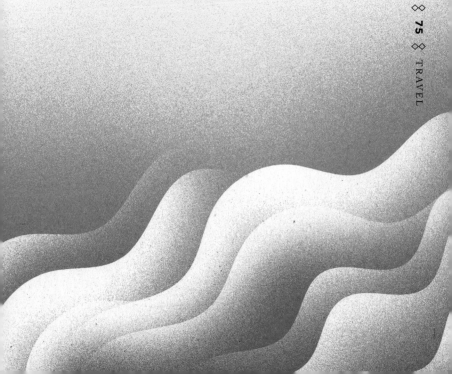

Hot-air Balloons

Up and away you float in your hot-air balloon. Light as feather, you drift through the air leaving all of your cares behind. This dream is about release. You may be feeling heavy of heart and weighed down with worry, but this is a sign that you're about to feel much lighter. Find ways to relax and clear the clutter in your life, both physical and emotional and you'll soon be walking on air.

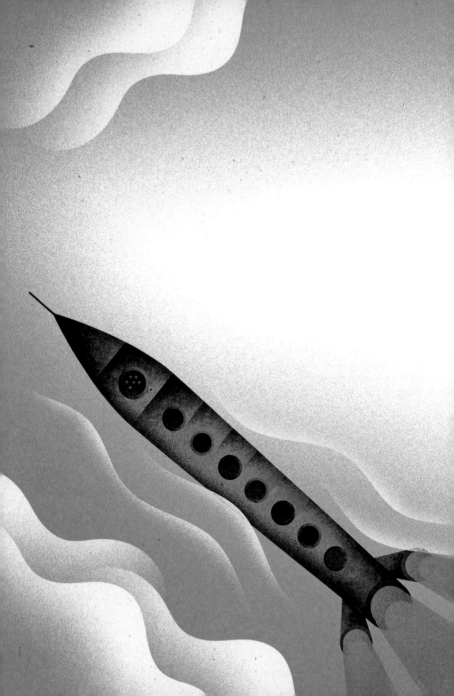

SPACE

◇◇◇

Space travel for everyone is the next frontier
in the human experience.
BUZZ ALDRIN

Aliens

Coming face to face with aliens might be unexpected, but in the dream realm anything is possible! In general, something described as alien is unknown to us but that doesn't mean it's a bad thing. If the aliens are friendly then trust your instincts, everything will be fine. If they're aggressive, then it's a sign your fears are overwhelming you. Anxiety prevents you from moving forwards, but this is only temporary. You have to come down to Earth at some point. You may be struggling to overcome your fears but will work through them eventually.

Earth

If you find yourself looking back at Earth from space, then your dream is telling you that you need to take a step back and see the bigger picture. You're too caught up in a drama to be objective. Another interpretation suggests that you've been limiting yourself in some way and need to broaden your horizons. It's time to step outside your comfort zone and try a different approach.

Moon

If the mystical Moon made its presence felt in your
dream, then it's time to trust your intuition. Whether
moonwalking or just gazing upon this luminescent orb,
the message is the same: take note of your feelings and
any insights that come to you at this time. The Moon
is associated with illumination and has been revered
throughout the ages. The ancients worshipped lunar deities
and looked to the Moon for inspiration. When the Moon
appears in dreams it's a clear sign that you're at the height
of creativity, so make the most of it!

Spaceships

Deep space is a strange place to find yourself when you're supposed to be sleeping, but it's also exciting and tells of adventures to come. If you're not already, you'll soon be breaking new ground, striking out on your own and making your mark. It's important to note whether you are a passenger or crew member. If the former, you'll be swept up in the action with little or no say in what's happening. As a crew member you'll be working with others to achieve your dreams. However, if you're the captain of the ship, then you need to take charge in order to fulfil your destiny.

Stars

Are you looking up at the stars? Perhaps you're sharing a special moment with someone you love beneath them, or simply alone in the dark, with only the night sky for company. Stars symbolize achievement and recognition. You are closer to achieving your dreams than you think. The stars above may seem out of reach, but you can see them shining brightly. You may feel on your own beneath the inky veil of night, but don't give up hope. Your lucky star is shining down on you.

WILD ANIMALS

People's hearts are like wild animals.
ALI IBN ALI TALIB

Bear

Big and bristly, the bear is a formidable character both
in real life and in dreams. Shamans in many traditions
associate this creature with healing and restoration because
it hibernates. If your dream puts you face to face with this
powerful animal, then you need to find courage in your
waking world. You may first need to gather your strength
and spend some time reflecting on what you really want,
then when you are ready stand firm and face up to reality.

Spider

Weavers of fate, spiders are feared by some and revered by others. To the ancients they were associated with wisdom, and able to spin the threads of destiny as intricately as their own webs. If a spider takes centre stage in your dream, it's a sign that change is on its way. Your life may take an unexpected turn, and while you may not be expecting the events that follow, you will make the most of them and find your true path. You could already be caught up in a drama that seems to be spiralling out of control, but the presence of a spider shows that you will take back the power and find balance once more.

WILD ANIMALS

Deer

The gentle deer has an innocence that is both
beautiful and fragile. If she visits your dreams,
it is a lovely omen, and a sign that you are loved
and cared for. Deer are often associated with fear,
because of the way they flee from danger.

Is there something you're afraid of?
If so, think of ways to channel that
fear into something positive and
move forwards. Even if the deer in
your dreams runs away, you don't
have to. She may be fleet of foot,
but you are fleet of mind
– and resourceful.

Wolf

Mysterious and elusive, the wolf knows how to survive in the wild. If you find one in your dreams, then you too have those sharp instincts. You're resilient and resourceful when you need to be. If the wolf stands on his own, then it's a sign that you also need to find your feet and spend some time in quiet contemplation before acting. If he's with his pack, then it's time to run with your own tribe. Get together with family and friends and make an effort to be sociable.

Horse

Something you're doing requires stamina and strength, which is why a horse has made its presence felt in your dream. Associated with power, longevity and going the distance, the appearance of a horse means you're about to, if you haven't already, begin a process which will take a huge amount of effort and tenacity. Whether you're riding, stroking or watching the horse, it's a sign that you will be successful.

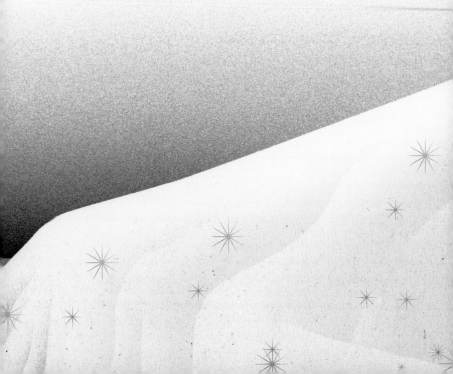

Snake

If a snake has slithered its way into your slumbers, don't panic! While some believe it is a negative omen, its real meaning is one of transformation. Just as the snake sheds its skin, you too are being urged to let go of something – this could be a preconceived idea or behaviour. Change the way you think, and you'll change the way you feel. If the snake in your dreams wraps itself around you, this suggests you are letting fear consume you. Believe in yourself. You have the power to transform your life.

Moth

Moths represent the shadow side of our personalities and the things we like to hide, from ourselves and others. While this is true, they are also drawn to light suggesting it is time to bring those things out in the open. Acknowledge your weaknesses and learn to love your true self. You might also hear or share a secret. Either way, something is going to come to light in the near future.

Butterfly

Graceful and delicate, butterflies are one of nature's wonders. This magical symbol suggests you're going through a period of change in your waking like. It may be gradual at first, but it is inevitable, so embrace it with open arms. In folklore the butterfly is associated with the spirit, and seeing one indicates spiritual enlightenment. You're being urged to find the beauty within and let it shine.

Birds

If you see birds in a dream, it's generally a positive
sign. If the birds are flying, singing or chirping, then
this indicates harmony and pleasant times ahead. If
the birds are pecking at you, then it's likely you feel
under attack in some way. This could be through
constant criticism, or nasty comments. The type
of bird is also symbolic. Blackbirds and robins
bring good fortune, crows carry wisdom, and
owls often represent the spirits of the dead
and can help you connect with
lost loved ones.

Bees

If industrious bee flies into your dreams then there are busy times ahead. You may already be in the thick of it, but don't try and do it all yourself. Whatever you want to achieve, you'll need to work as a team to get there. The ancients thought of the bee as a representation of the Sun and associated it with light and warmth. Whether you see a swarm of bees, have one land on you, or hold one in your hands, you're being given the gift of happiness and friendship.

PETS

◇◇◇

Our perfect companions never have fewer than four feet.
SIDONIE-GABRIELLE COLETTE

Cats

Since the beginning of time humans have fallen under the spell of felines. Enigmatic and mysterious, the cat is associated with magic, witchcraft and the fairy realm. If your dreams are filled with moggies, one or many, then you're being urged to look beyond the veil. Trust your intuition and follow your heart. You know what is right for you at this time, so be bold and take a leap of faith. If the cats in your dream are big cats, then consider what they represent. A lion suggests you need to be courageous, while a cheetah is known for its speed, so you need to act quickly.

Dogs

Throughout the world, dogs are seen as loyal companions, and if one visits your dream it's a sign that you too are a good friend. The dog could represent a close friend, or simply the idea of friendship being important to you. Dogs are also associated with protection, and their bark can be a warning sign. If the dog in your dream is barking loudly, it could be your subconscious telling you to tread carefully and be cautious in your interactions with others.

Rabbits

In China, rabbits are sacred and associated with the moon goddess Chang'e. The Celts believed they were messengers between this world and the next and could commune with spirits. Often thought of as tricksters for their quick thinking, rabbits signify opportunity. It's time to take a risk; good fortune is knocking at your door, but you must be ready to take a leap.

Guinea Pig

Guinea pigs represent responsibility; these cuddly creatures
have a sweet nature, so dreaming of one is a sign that
you too have a big heart and you're always willing to lend
a hand to those in need. On the negative side, this means
that responsibility is heaped upon you, and you can feel
overwhelmed at times. If you see something bad happen
to a guinea pig, this suggests you're concerned about
the welfare of someone.

Hamster

Dreaming of a hamster, particularly holding one in your
hands, suggests you're trying to handle a problem or you're
in the middle of a tricky situation. The best advice would be
to let it go and take a step back. The more you try to resolve
the situation at this time, the worse things will get. Space and
sensitivity are key here.

Mouse

To see a mouse, whether in a dream or real life, is considered
a positive omen. Good fortune is on its way, and while this
may not be a lottery win it will be a surprise that makes you
smile. If you're trying to catch the mouse and it's running
away from you, then this suggests minor complications that
relate to your career. Holding a mouse indicates an issue
that you're aware of and dealing with effectively.

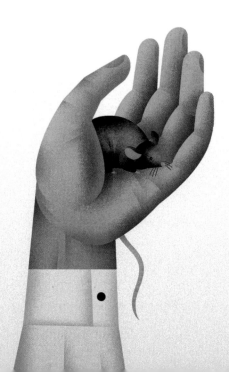

NATURE
&
NATURAL
WONDERS

◇◇◇

Be a good animal, true to your animal instincts.
D. H. LAWRENCE,
THE WHITE PEACOCK

Caring for Animals

To see yourself caring for an animal in a dream denotes
a compassionate personality. It is likely that in real life you're
being called to look after a person or situation, or perhaps
there's something that you need to nurture within yourself.
If you're caring for a pet, this suggests that you have a strong
bond, and the emotional connection between you transcends
any barriers to communication. It could be that you're
feeling overanxious about your pet, and this worry has
seeped into your dream.

Living with Animals

If you find you're enclosed in a space with a group of animals,
or living among them, it is important to note what kind of
animal they are and what they represent. If, for example,
you're trapped in a confined space with a pride of lions, but
they leave you unharmed, this suggests that you will face your
fear and realize that there was nothing to worry about. It also
suggests an affinity with these big cats, and that you need to
draw upon deep reserves of courage.

Turning into an Animal

In ancient times, tribes throughout the world looked to the animal kingdom for inspiration, strength and power. Animals were chosen for their specific skills and used as totems. This practice involved taking on the form and behaviour of the animal, by wearing its skin, or moving in a certain way to look like the creature. If you dream of turning into an animal, it's likely you feel an affinity with it, and even want to develop similar characteristics and traits. Consider what the animal represents and make a list of qualities, then see if any resonate with you.

Woodland Adventures

Finding yourself alone in the woods or exploring the countryside is a good sign. Nature has a calming influence on mind, body and soul, and this indicates a need for peace, and finding new ways to de-stress. If the woods are dark and foreboding, then it's your subconscious telling you to delve deep, there's something you need to face and work through on an emotional level. Once you've done this, you'll find the inner peace you crave.

Mountains and hills

If you find yourself looking up at a hill or mountain,
this suggests there's a task in front of you, something
you're facing which you may have reservations about.
If you can see the top, then success is likely. If the peak
is out of view, then you're unsure about the final outcome.
If you're already climbing the hill, then you're probably in
the thick of it and already working towards your goal. To
find yourself standing at the summit is a good sign: you're
in a position of power and feel elevated in some way. It's
time to celebrate this victory.

Rainbows

To behold a rainbow in a dream is highly auspicious.
This symbol of good fortune brings blessings and general
happiness. If you've been going through a rough patch
or feeling unwell the rainbow is a sign that things are about
to change for the better. You're coming to the end of this
period, and the future looks bright. Often associated with
abundance, the rainbow suggests that any issues around
money will also be resolved.

Waterfalls

The waterfall always finds a way to flow over the rocks. If one
pops up in your dream it's a sign that you also need to find
your own way. You may be restricted in some way, or facing
obstacles, but that doesn't mean you can't achieve your goal.
Be flexible like the waterfall and find a new path. A symbol
of spiritual rejuvenation, the waterfall also suggests a need
for peace and harmony. You may experience an awakening
in some area of your life.

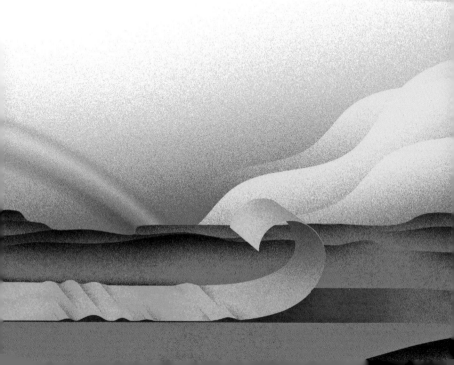

MYSTICAL CREATURES

… and from the heart of the blossom there appeared a unicorn.
JAMES ENDICOTT

Dragon

In the traditions of the East the dragon is a fortunate omen and a symbol of wealth and success, while the West takes a more cautious approach. To them the dragon is vengeful and often destructive. To dream of a dragon is a sign that you're about to step into the limelight in some way. You could take on a leadership role or start a new venture. Whatever you decide to do, fortune is on your side. You may have to defend your decision in some way, but your natural charm will win people over.

Phoenix

A symbol of rebirth and new beginnings, when a phoenix shows up in your dream it means you're starting a new cycle. One door may be closing, but another is about to open. The past is the past, and it's time to move forward with optimism. You may have made mistakes, but you've learned from them, and this fresh start gives you the chance to use the knowledge you've gained.

Mermaid

This beautiful hybrid from myth and legend, represents
feminine strength and is associated with the emotions.
To see one in your dreams suggests you're feeling emotional
and could be oversensitive about some area of your life. Love
may be on the cards, and passionate feelings come out of
the blue to consume you. To dream you are a mermaid is
a warning not to get too caught up in the romance of it all.
Take care of your heart and keep a level head.

Unicorn

Throughout folklore the unicorn is seen as a symbol of hope, purity and love. Wherever it goes, it spreads a little magic. To see one in a dream is a wonderful omen. You'll soon be on cloud nine and bursting with happiness. Love is the key to this dream, and new love or a deepening connection is on the horizon. Open your heart and share how you feel with your nearest and dearest. It's time to celebrate your relationships.

ROMANCE & DATING

◇◇◇

True love stories never have endings.
RICHARD BACH

Soulmate

Should you dream of meeting your soulmate, whether they are known to you or a complete stranger, the meaning is the same. This person represents you, and all the qualities you have. When you meet your perfect partner in your dreams, what you're actually doing is coming face to face with yourself. This dream is about learning to love who you are. You may already be doing this in your waking life, but a period of personal growth and self-acceptance is ahead.

Falling in Love

If you dream you're falling in love, then you're yearning for some kind of connection. If you're already in a relationship, then you could be craving the closeness you first felt when you got together. If you're single, it could be a deeper longing for affection and to meet someone special. If the person is known to you, then it suggests that you'd like to strengthen existing relationships, whether they're based on friendship or romantic attraction.

Going on a Date

If you're actively dating, then it's no surprise you might dream of going on a date. This is your brain's way of preparing you for the real thing, in the form of an imaginary rehearsal. You may have anxieties about dating, which is why it is at the forefront of your mind. If the date is with a stranger and all goes well, this suggests you're on a journey of self-discovery. You're getting to know your strengths and talents. A disastrous date means there's some part of yourself that you don't like or feel comfortable with.

Breaking Up

To dream you're splitting up with your current partner denotes a deep-seated fear of rejection. You're feeling vulnerable in the relationship, but this is mostly down to a lack of self-esteem, rather than anything tangible. Instead of worrying incessantly about the future, start living in the present. Enjoy the time you spend together, but also the precious time spent apart. Learn to love yourself and dreams like this will fade.

Passionate Affair

If you dream you're having an affair, then this often means you're experiencing a power struggle between what you feel is right, and your deeper desires. You know what is socially acceptable, but you're feeling tempted in some way. If you're in a relationship, then you could be feeling bored and long to inject some excitement into your usual routine.

One-night Stand

If your dream finds you having a brief fling with a complete stranger, then this suggests you're tempted to throw caution to the wind. This could be a good thing, if you're the type of person that always sticks to the rules and needs to be more spontaneous, however, there's an element of danger here. Deep down, you know there's a risk involved. You need to weigh up whether it's worth it or not.

Dreaming of an Ex

Dreaming of getting together with an old flame is a sign that you are missing companionship. Even if you're in a new relationship, there may be something about the old one that you miss. If you still hold a torch for your ex, then the dream is quite literal, but it doesn't mean you'll get back with this person. It's a reflection of how you're feeling at this time. Sometimes there can be guilt or unfinished business from past romances and this can surface in this type of dream.

Proposal

To analyze this dream, you need to look at a
number of factors. Who is doing the proposing, and
what is the outcome? Does the proposal come from
your current partner, or a stranger? If you're the
one being to proposed to by your partner, then this
shows an underlying need for commitment. You
hope this relationship will go the distance. If it's
a stranger, then it suggests either you haven't found
the one yet, or you need to find some aspect of
yourself to feel complete. If you're proposing, then
there's something you want which will help you
feel more secure. You know what it is, you just
need to ask for it.

Wedding Dress

If you're wearing a wedding dress in your dream, this suggests you're searching for something or someone to make you feel special. On a deeper level you could be looking for your place in the world, or perhaps you don't feel you fit with your current social group. If it's the dress of your dreams, then you're wishing for something that might appear to be out of reach at the moment, but that doesn't mean you should give up – you will get there eventually. If you hate the dress, this suggests you feel stuck in a horrible situation that you'd like to get out of. If it doesn't fit properly, then there's something in your life which doesn't fit on an emotional level.

Ceremony

If you're going through a wedding ceremony in your dream, then there's something you want to reaffirm in your life. In general, this is a positive and harmonious sign. You're satisfied and feeling in control. Everything is in balance. Even if you're not quite at this stage yet, you will be soon, so relax and enjoy this peaceful period.

Ring

The ring, whether for an engagement or a wedding, is a symbol of commitment. It says, 'We're together and we're in it for the long haul.' In reality this could indicate you're about to enter into an agreement with someone, either on a personal or professional level. You're close to sealing the deal, but you still need to check all the finer details. If the ring is big and flashy then approach with caution, the situation might not be all it seems. If you love the ring, then matters will go well and you'll be happy with the outcome. If the ring is lost, then the deal may not live up to your expectations; make sure you have a plan B.

Jilted Speeches

Whether you're being jilted at the altar or a current partner leaves you in your dream, the underlying theme is one of abandonment. You could already be feeling let down in some way or you're worried that this is about to happen. There's a level of embarrassment that comes with this, and it may be that you feel that someone is making fun of you or doesn't respect you. If you're the one doing the jilting then it's likely that you reject something about your current partner, this could be an opinion or a behaviour that you don't agree with.

Wedding Cake

Cutting the wedding cake is something newlyweds usually do together, it's the first step on their journey into married life. Doing this in a dream is a sign that you're on the right path. You're in a happy place and feel relaxed with the way everything is going. Eating the cake indicates you're enjoying life at the moment, but if you eat too much or make a mess, then it's a warning not to take things to excess. Have fun but look after yourself and those around you.

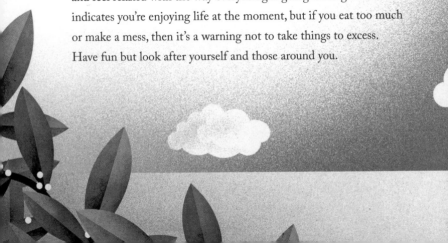

FAMILY

◇◇◇

A happy family is but an earlier heaven.
GEORGE BERNARD SHAW

Dreaming of Family Members

Dreaming of family and friends can be a positive experience. To interpret the dream correctly you need to consider a number of factors, including what you're doing in the dream, and how you feel. If you're having a disagreement, then this could indicate you need to examine your communication with others and how you approach issues. Enjoying time together shows you feel happy and settled in your life. If you and your family are under threat, then you're feeling protective towards your nearest and dearest.

Birthdays
and Celebrations

To dream it's your birthday is a positive sign. You're feeling
on top of the world. You've emerged from a period of
struggle and you're about to get the recognition you deserve.
Wishes that you've held close to your heart are about to be
realized, and you'll reap the rewards for past efforts. This is
also the perfect time to reinvent yourself in some way. Any
kind of family celebration is a good omen and brings new
opportunities your way.

Pregnancy

Being pregnant is to be fertile and ready to give birth to new life. In reality, this sense of expectancy comes in many shapes and forms, from being full of new ideas or about to launch a creative project, to simply having joie de vivre and a renewed sense of enthusiasm. You could be waiting for something to take off, or about to realize your full potential. If the pregnancy goes well, then your plans will be successful. If you're sick, then it suggests feelings of frustration; you want to get your ideas out quickly, but it's not possible. Bide your time and know that the period of gestation is essential for a positive outcome.

Childbirth

You are entering a new phase when you dream about giving birth. It doesn't necessarily mean you'll have a baby unless you're already pregnant. Most likely you're about to launch a new project, idea, or put a cherished plan into action. There will be some effort involved, as there is in actual childbirth, but it will be worth it in the end. Giving birth to twins or triplets, suggests a busy creative period where you'll be buzzing with ideas. If your offspring is unexpected, don't panic; this is also a good sign and indicates a few surprises along the way.

Death

While dreaming of your death can be disturbing, it is not an ill omen. Death comes in many forms, and it's likely that you're getting ready to close a door and move on to a new chapter in your life. There will be an ending of sorts, but it is expected and there will be a sense of satisfaction that you are now able to move forwards. If your dream is of a loved one passing away, then this suggests something may be lost between you. The relationship you have is changing, or it could literally mean that there is physical distance between you, i.e. they have moved away or are planning on living elsewhere.

Funeral

To see or participate in a funeral, is a sign that you're trying to bury something. This could be a secret, a fear, or some kind of worry. It's also a sign that your feelings are repressed. As funerals are so often serious and sombre, it suggests a general sadness in all you do. Look at your waking life and what is making you feel so drained. Make a list of all the things you can do that lift your spirits and make a point of doing at least one of them every day.

Lost Loved Ones

In many cultures, dreaming of those who have passed away
is thought to be a spiritual sign and a way in which the spirits
can communicate with those still living. These dreams are
incredibly vivid, and the emotions experienced may influence
us for days afterwards. The presence of a lost loved one in
a dream is extremely comforting and often happens when
we need reassurance or strength in our daily life. If they say
something to you, consider what it means and how it relates
to your waking world, as this is a powerful message from your
subconscious mind.

WORK
& STUDY

◇◇◇

Study the past, if you would divine the future.
CONFUCIUS

Taking Exams

When we are tested in dreams, it follows that we have similar feelings in our waking life. You may feel under pressure at work, anxious about your performance, or simply that someone is judging you. It could be that you are working towards a specific goal but feel unprepared in some way. Look to the conditions of the test for a deeper interpretation. If you are stressed and have problems either with the content or physical circumstances, this points to a lack of knowledge and confidence. You may need to put extra effort into reaching your career goals. If the exam goes well then you are ready to take the lead in some way and show those that matter how much you can achieve.

Being Interviewed

This type of dream often occurs when we have some kind of test or appraisal that we're preparing for in real life. If this is not the case, then the dream is usually a positive sign. Your efforts have been noticed and you will soon reap the rewards. While interviews can be nerve-racking, it also suggests that you'll be given the opportunity to make the most of your talents and shine. Work changes are afoot, but they bring much deserved success.

Giving a Presentation

Public speaking is a common dream scenario and usually indicates a need to get something off your chest. You may be having trouble expressing your needs, at work or in your personal life. If you feel nervous in the dream, then you could be afraid of how you're being perceived by colleagues and peers and this is holding you back in some way. Struggling to find the right words indicates a need to speak up for yourself and address a situation that is bothering you. Take your time and write down what you want to say so that you're properly prepared. If the presentation is a success, then this shows you're in a good place and able to communicate effectively, so make the most of this and use your silver tongue to ask for a pay rise or promotion.

Being late for work

There's an underlying feeling of frustration with this dream. You want to be somewhere you're not, and it doesn't matter how hard you try you can't seem to get there. Whether you're stuck in traffic, or simply can't get to or find your office, this dream suggests you feel like you're missing out on something. There's a sense that time is running out in relation to one particular dream or goal, but this is only your perception.

Starting a New Job

The first day at a new job can be daunting, and if this crops up in your dreams then it suggests you're facing a new challenge. You know you can't avoid it, but the thought of it is weighing on your mind. Sometimes this dream can mean you feel a bit like an outsider, the new person within a team where everyone knows each other. There's a sense of vulnerability with this dream, but also a feeling of hope. You do not know what's around the corner, so stop fearing what's ahead, embrace it and look to the future with optimism.

Getting a Promotion

When this type of dream makes an appearance, it's a sign of abundance to come. Good things are on their way, particularly when it comes to work and cherished ambitions. You may already feel you deserve a promotion, or recognition for your efforts. If this is not forthcoming at the moment, it will be soon. This dream also suggests you've taken on extra responsibility, personally or professionally. You may feel like you had no choice in the matter, but your willingness to help has earned brownie points which will make a difference to your future.

Getting a Pay Rise

The difference between dreaming about getting a pay rise
and a promotion is that the former is primarily about
money and security, while the latter relates to status and
aspirations. To see your bank balance increase in this way
suggests that financial matters are at the forefront of your
mind. You may be worried about money, and feel you need
to generate more income. This dream can also mean that
you're looking to establish some security in your life, in
which case this is a positive sign. You're about to enter
a stable and prosperous period.

Being the Boss

If you're already in a management role and you dream about this, then it's a sign you need to step up a gear and take the lead. You're being called to action! If you aren't the boss but dream you are then it indicates a need to take control. You have the power to create the future, so visualize what you want and where you want to be and then take the steps you need to get there. Consider how you felt during the dream too. If being the boss made you feel good then it suggests you're ready to take on more responsibility at work. If you found it hard to discipline colleagues and make the right decisions, then your self-esteem may need a boost.

Work Problems / Issues

When work issues take over your dreams there's one simple explanation; you're overworked and exhausted. You could be obsessing about a particular project or focusing on mistakes you've made instead of recognizing more positive attributes. Sometimes this type of dream indicates a period of hard work to come, where you will have to step up and deal with tricky issues. Either way, work is at the forefront of your mind. Consider what you can do in your waking world to de-stress and find some peace at the end of the working day.

Colleagues

If one or more of your work colleagues makes an appearance, then this hints at work issues that need to be resolved. This may be with the people in your dream, or not. Work is definitely on your mind, even if you're trying not to focus on it. This type of dream also points towards working relationships and how you get on with your colleagues. If you harbour feelings of resentment or anger, these will surface in the dream, as will more positive emotions. The dream could also indicate that you need to work as a team to achieve your goals, rather than going it alone.

Work Events

To see yourself at a social event with work colleagues implies that you feel comfortable with your peers. You've been accepted into the group and enjoy working with them and sharing ideas. This is a good place for you to be, and you'll thrive in this position. If you're about to start a new job, this suggests that all will go well. You'll fit in with the team and enjoy working with them. New prospects are on the horizon, and you could meet someone who will be influential through friends. Be open and ready to seize any opportunity that comes your way!

Losing your Job

Dreaming that you've lost your job is a sign that you're feeling anxious about some area of your life. This doesn't necessarily have to be work-related, you could be feeling insecure in a relationship, or even be worrying about money. How you lose the job also has some bearing. If you're fired, this suggests you feel cut off in some way and you could have anger issues which relate to this. Redundancy implies some kind of rejection. You may feel that your ideas and opinions will be discarded, or that you are surplus to requirements.

Struggling to Find a Job

If your dream sees you struggling to find work, then this relates to your personal identity, how you see and value yourself. You might think you don't deserve something, and in doing so, find you're constantly facing setbacks. The struggle could also be internal, you're battling emotions and negative thoughts. This dream suggests you need to switch perspective and focus on the positive things in your life.

An Old Job

If you find yourself going back in time to a previous job in your dream, this suggests you need to look back into the past in order to move forwards. You could be repeating a cycle of behaviour, or even find yourself in a situation you've been in before. This dream suggests there's a lesson you need to learn, and you can only do this by examining the past. An alternative interpretation would be that there's something from the past that you're still yearning for, this could be a job, friendship, or a relationship. Now is the time to fully cut those ties and look to the future with optimism.

Starting your Own Business

If you see yourself as an entrepreneur setting up your own business, then this means your plans for the future are well-starred. You're going through a creative phase and you feel inspired. If you're not already starting a new project, you will be soon. Be prepared for a period of frenetic activity which will see you rising to new heights. This dream also suggests a need to go it alone and stand out from the crowd. It's time to walk your own path in life!

Changing Careers

To dream of a career change can be indicative of how you really feel about your current role. Deep down, you may have a desire to do something completely different, and this is surfacing in your dreams. If you're happy in your job and this dream pops up then the change you seek might not be career-related. It could be that you need to reinvent yourself in some way; this could be as simple as a rejuvenating makeover, or something more in depth, such as rethinking your belief system, behaviour and attitude. This dream often arises out of boredom, so look to your current situation and be honest about how you feel, then look at the things you can change to make you feel better.

LAST WORD

✧✧✧

*The future belongs to those who believe
in the beauty of their dreams.*
ELEANOR ROOSEVELT

Your dreams are a gift.

They offer an insight into what you truly think and feel, and help you process events in the real world.

They provide inspiration, and a place for your imagination to play. They can even help you work through tricky situations and rehearse real life events in the safety and comfort of your slumbers.

The symbols and scenarios covered here are a starting point, but the real magic comes from within. Follow your heart, and let your dreams do the rest.

PUBLISHING DIRECTOR Sarah Lavelle
COMMISSIONING EDITOR Harriet Butt
DESIGNER Maeve Bargman
ILLUSTRATOR Jesús Sotés Vicente
PRODUCTION DIRECTOR Vincent Smith
PRODUCTION CONTROLLER Nikolaus Ginelli

Published in 2019 by Quadrille, an imprint of
Hardie Grant Publishing

QUADRILLE
52–54 Southwark Street
London SE1 1UN
quadrille.com

Cataloguing in Publication Data: a catalogue record for this
book is available from the British Library.

text © Alison Davies 2019
illustrations © Jesús Sotés Vicente 2019
design © Quadrille 2019

ISBN 978 1 78713 339 6
Printed in China